INTRODUCTION

This book is about probation. In North Carolina, probation is a form of punishment in which a defendant can avoid going to prison by complying with a set of conditions imposed by the sentencing judge. If the probation is supervised, the defendant will have a probation officer—an employee of the North Carolina Department of Public Safety who monitors the case and reports violations to the judge. Probation can also be used to monitor a person's compliance with a diversion program like a deferred prosecution or conditional discharge (for example, "90-96," a diversionary option for certain drug crimes).

Probation is not to be confused with post-release supervision or parole. Those are supervision periods that *follow* a person's release from prison, and which are managed by the Post-Release Supervision and Parole Commission in Raleigh, not by the courts. Probation comes *before* a term of imprisonment. In fact, if a person does well on probation, he or she will never go to prison at all.

This is the second issue in a series of graphic novels explaining North Carolina's sentencing laws. Presenting the information in illustrated form is by no means intended to make light of a serious topic. It is, rather, offered as an accessible way to explain a complicated subject. It is meant to give crime victims, defendants, inmates, probationers, and their families an understandable resource that translates the words and numbers on a sentencing judgment into a practical reality. I hope it will be useful to judges, lawyers, and probation officers, too.

I do not have artistic talent to create something like this on my own. Jason Whitley, a brilliant designer who works at the Eshelman School of Pharmacy at UNC–Chapel Hill, illustrated the book. Chad Owens, Senior Policy Administrator for Probation for the North Carolina Division of Adult Correction and Juvenile Justice, co-authored the text, ensuring that the book accurately describes how probationary sentences are administered. I thank both of them for their essential contributions. I am also grateful to Kevin Justice, Melissa Twomey, and Owen DuBose for their work producing this book. Any errors in the text are my own.

Jamie Markham
Chapel Hill
September 2019

STORY BY:
JAMIE MARKHAM
AND CHAD OWENS

ART BY:
JASON WHITLEY

1

IN NORTH CAROLINA, A SENTENCE TO SUPERVISED PROBATION HAS TWO PARTS: **THE SUPERVISION PERIOD** AND THE **SUSPENDED TERM OF IMPRISONMENT**.

THE SUPERVISION PERIOD IS THE LENGTH OF TIME THE DEFENDANT IS SUPERVISED BY A PROBATION OFFICER IN THE COMMUNITY, DURING WHICH HE OR SHE MUST FOLLOW CONDITIONS SET BY THE JUDGE. IN THIS CASE, THE SUPERVISION PERIOD IS **36 MONTHS**.

THE SUSPENDED TERM OF IMPRISONMENT IS THE SENTENCE THE DEFENDANT WILL SERVE IF HE OR SHE FAILS ON PROBATION AND GETS REVOKED. THE SUSPENDED SENTENCE IS SOMETIMES SAID TO "HANG OVER THE DEFENDANT'S HEAD" DURING THE PERIOD OF PROBATION. IN THIS CASE, THE SUSPENDED TERM OF IMPRISONMENT IS 10-21 MONTHS.

THE LONGEST PERIOD OF PROBATION A JUDGE CAN IMPOSE AT SENTENCING IN NORTH CAROLINA IS FIVE YEARS. THE AVERAGE PROBATION PERIOD FOR A FELONY IS 26 MONTHS.

THE TIME SPENT UNDER SUPERVISION IN THE COMMUNITY DOES NOT IN ANY WAY COUNT FOR CREDIT AGAINST THE TERM OF IMPRISONMENT. A PERSON REVOKED ON THE LAST DAY OF HIS OR HER SUPERVISION PERIOD COULD STILL BE REQUIRED TO SERVE THE FULL TERM OF IMPRISONMENT.

10-21 MONTHS

36 MONTHS

THE DEFENDANT'S FIRST STOP AFTER SENTENCING WILL BE **INTAKE** WITH A JUDICIAL SERVICES COORDINATOR (JSC), AN EMPLOYEE OF THE PROBATION DEPARTMENT. THE JSC GATHERS BIOGRAPHICAL INFORMATION, REVIEWS THE CONDITIONS OF PROBATION, AND ASSIGNS THE DEFENDANT TO A SUPERVISING PROBATION OFFICER IN THE COUNTY WHERE HE OR SHE RESIDES.

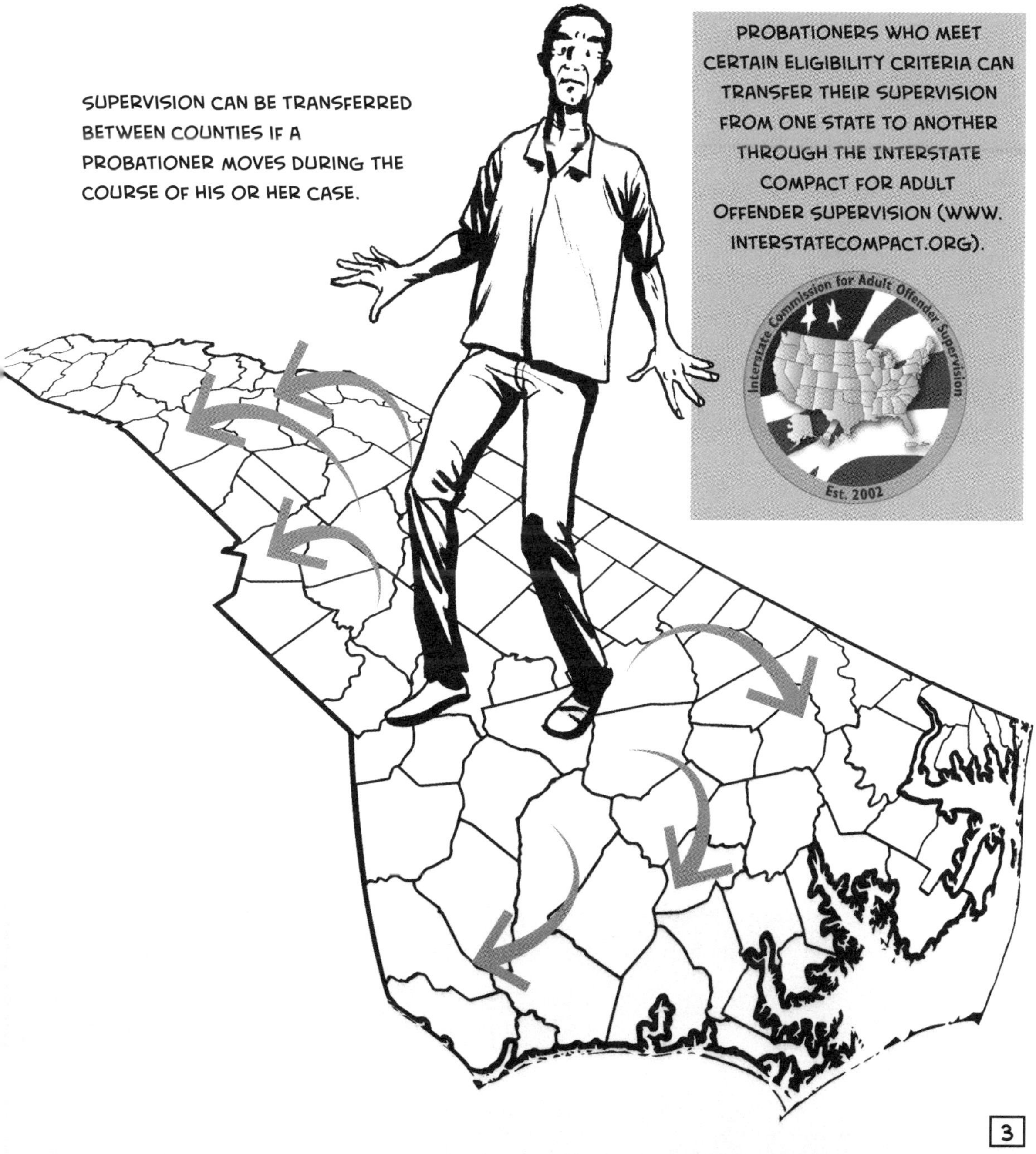

SUPERVISION CAN BE TRANSFERRED BETWEEN COUNTIES IF A PROBATIONER MOVES DURING THE COURSE OF HIS OR HER CASE.

PROBATIONERS WHO MEET CERTAIN ELIGIBILITY CRITERIA CAN TRANSFER THEIR SUPERVISION FROM ONE STATE TO ANOTHER THROUGH THE INTERSTATE COMPACT FOR ADULT OFFENDER SUPERVISION (WWW. INTERSTATECOMPACT.ORG).

Interstate Commission for Adult Offender Supervision

Est. 2002

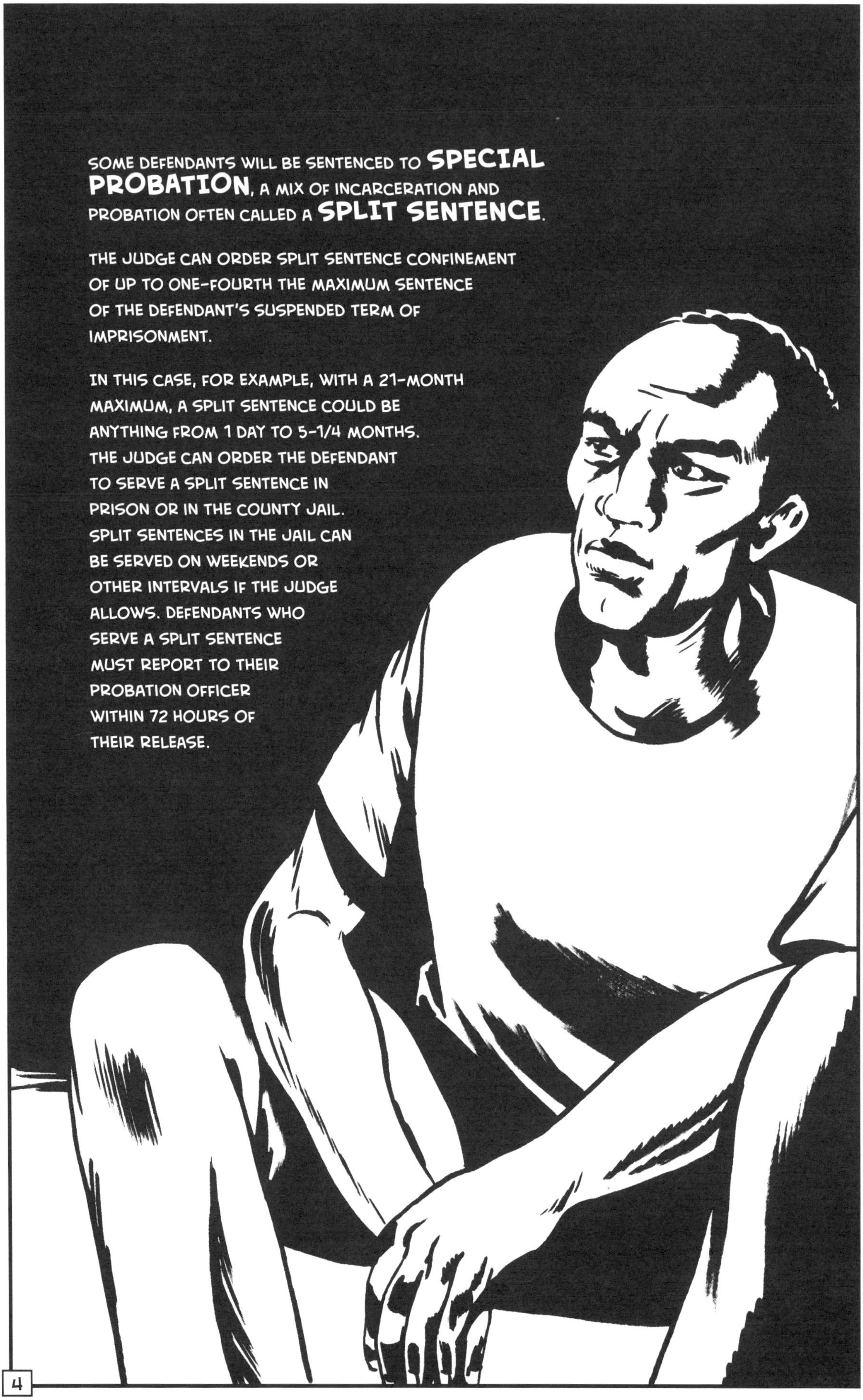

SOME DEFENDANTS WILL BE SENTENCED TO **SPECIAL PROBATION**, A MIX OF INCARCERATION AND PROBATION OFTEN CALLED A **SPLIT SENTENCE**.

THE JUDGE CAN ORDER SPLIT SENTENCE CONFINEMENT OF UP TO ONE-FOURTH THE MAXIMUM SENTENCE OF THE DEFENDANT'S SUSPENDED TERM OF IMPRISONMENT.

IN THIS CASE, FOR EXAMPLE, WITH A 21-MONTH MAXIMUM, A SPLIT SENTENCE COULD BE ANYTHING FROM 1 DAY TO 5-1/4 MONTHS. THE JUDGE CAN ORDER THE DEFENDANT TO SERVE A SPLIT SENTENCE IN PRISON OR IN THE COUNTY JAIL. SPLIT SENTENCES IN THE JAIL CAN BE SERVED ON WEEKENDS OR OTHER INTERVALS IF THE JUDGE ALLOWS. DEFENDANTS WHO SERVE A SPLIT SENTENCE MUST REPORT TO THEIR PROBATION OFFICER WITHIN 72 HOURS OF THEIR RELEASE.

A PROBATIONER WILL REPORT TO HIS OR HER SUPERVISING PROBATION OFFICER IN THE COUNTY OF RESIDENCE SOON AFTER MEETING WITH THE JSC OR FINISHING A SPLIT SENTENCE.

AT THAT FIRST MEETING, THE PROBATION OFFICER WILL EXPLAIN THE GENERAL EXPECTATIONS OF PROBATION, REVIEW A COPY OF THE SENTENCING JUDGMENT, AND EXPLAIN THE CONSEQUENCES OF NONCOMPLIANCE.

DURING THE **FIRST MONTH** OF SUPERVISION, THE PROBATION OFFICER WILL VISIT THE PROBATIONER'S RESIDENCE.

THE OFFICER WILL DO A WALKTHROUGH OF THE RESIDENCE AND INFORM THE PROBATIONER AND OTHER RESIDENTS ABOUT THE CONDITIONS OF SUPERVISION,

INCLUDING THE AUTHORITY TO CONDUCT A WARRANTLESS SEARCH OF THE RESIDENCE.

THE FIRST 60 DAYS

WITHIN THE FIRST 60 DAYS OF A PERSON'S PROBATION, THE OFFICER WILL COMPLETE AN ASSESSMENT PROCESS KNOWN AS THE RISK-NEEDS ASSESSMENT, OR RNA. THE RNA IS MADE UP OF TWO PARTS: A RISK ASSESSMENT (IT'S CALLED THE "OFFENDER TRAITS INVENTORY-REVISED" OR OTI-R) AND A NEEDS ASSESSMENT THAT INCLUDES A QUESTIONNAIRE COMPLETED BY THE PROBATIONER (THE "OFFENDER SELF-REPORT") AND AN INTERVIEW COMPLETED BY THE PROBATION OFFICER (THE "OFFICER INTERVIEW AND IMPRESSIONS"). THE RISK ASSESSMENT PREDICTS A PERSON'S LIKELIHOOD OF REOFFENDING, WHILE THE NEEDS ASSESSMENT IDENTIFIES THINGS LIKE FAMILY ISSUES, SUBSTANCE ABUSE, AND OTHER FACTORS THAT CONTRIBUTE TO CRIMINAL BEHAVIOR.

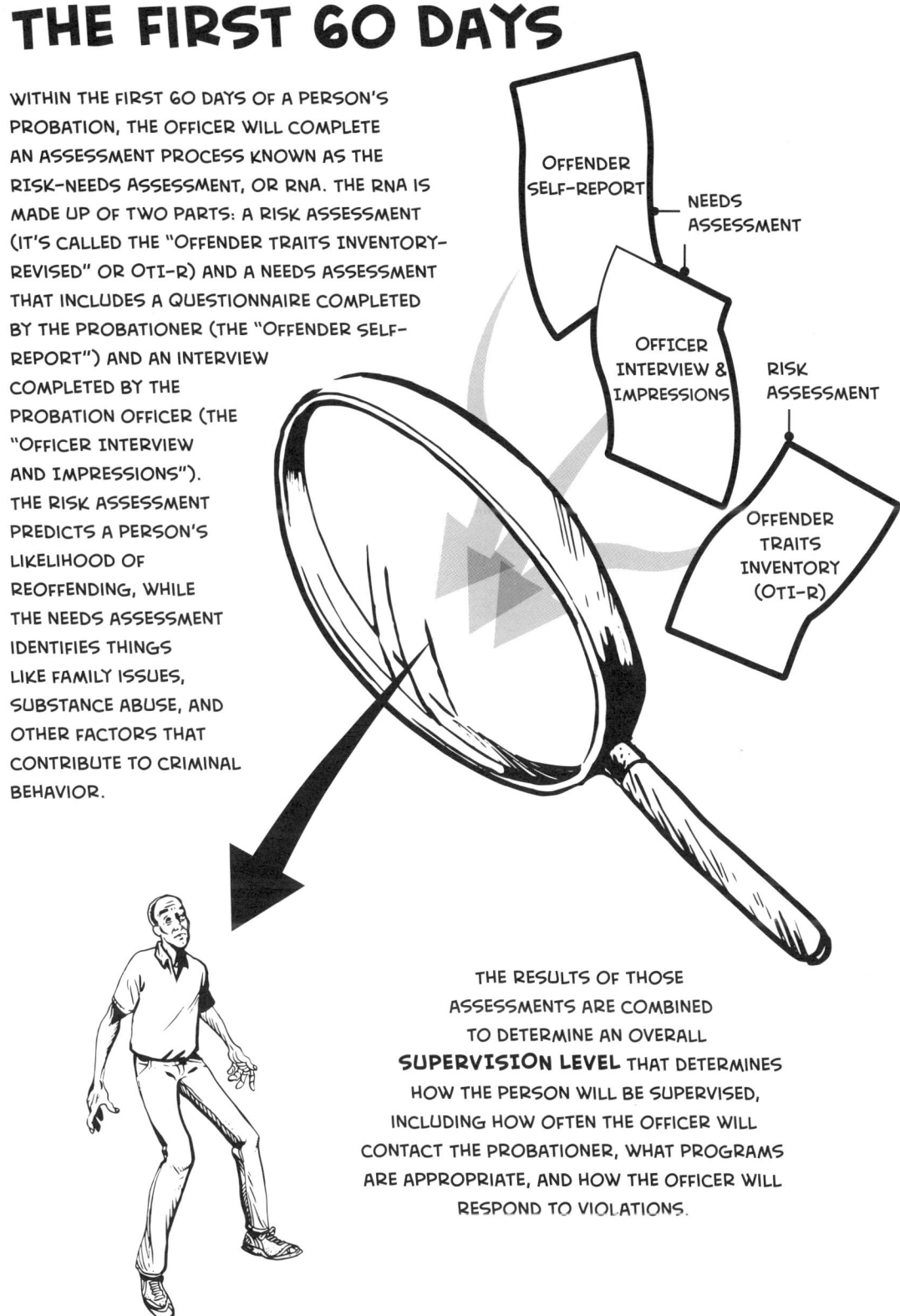

OFFENDER SELF-REPORT

NEEDS ASSESSMENT

OFFICER INTERVIEW & IMPRESSIONS

RISK ASSESSMENT

OFFENDER TRAITS INVENTORY (OTI-R)

THE RESULTS OF THOSE ASSESSMENTS ARE COMBINED TO DETERMINE AN OVERALL **SUPERVISION LEVEL** THAT DETERMINES HOW THE PERSON WILL BE SUPERVISED, INCLUDING HOW OFTEN THE OFFICER WILL CONTACT THE PROBATIONER, WHAT PROGRAMS ARE APPROPRIATE, AND HOW THE OFFICER WILL RESPOND TO VIOLATIONS.

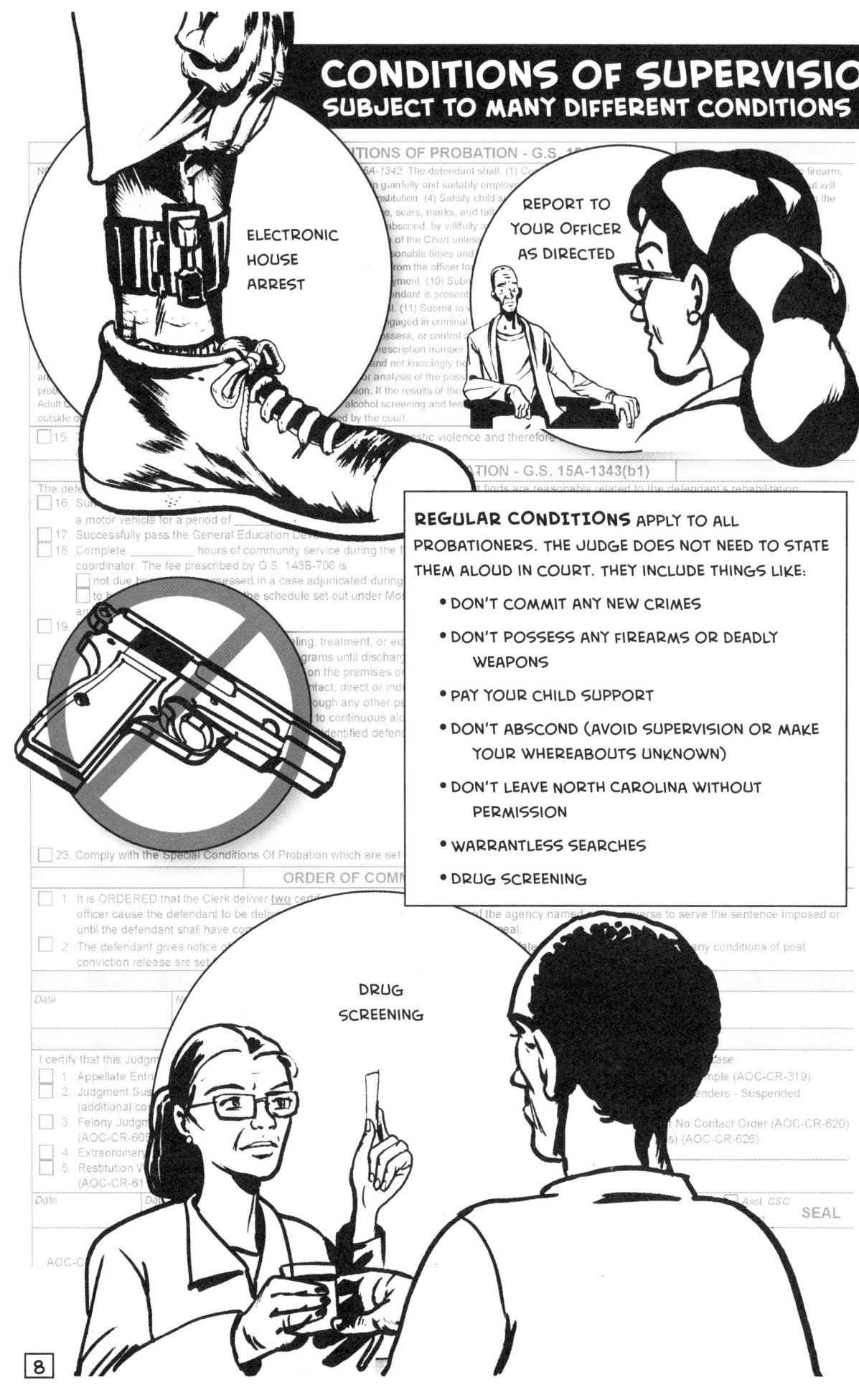

CONDITIONS OF SUPERVISIO
SUBJECT TO MANY DIFFERENT CONDITIONS

ELECTRONIC HOUSE ARREST

REPORT TO YOUR OFFICER AS DIRECTED

REGULAR CONDITIONS APPLY TO ALL PROBATIONERS. THE JUDGE DOES NOT NEED TO STATE THEM ALOUD IN COURT. THEY INCLUDE THINGS LIKE:

- DON'T COMMIT ANY NEW CRIMES
- DON'T POSSESS ANY FIREARMS OR DEADLY WEAPONS
- PAY YOUR CHILD SUPPORT
- DON'T ABSCOND (AVOID SUPERVISION OR MAKE YOUR WHEREABOUTS UNKNOWN)
- DON'T LEAVE NORTH CAROLINA WITHOUT PERMISSION
- WARRANTLESS SEARCHES
- DRUG SCREENING

DRUG SCREENING

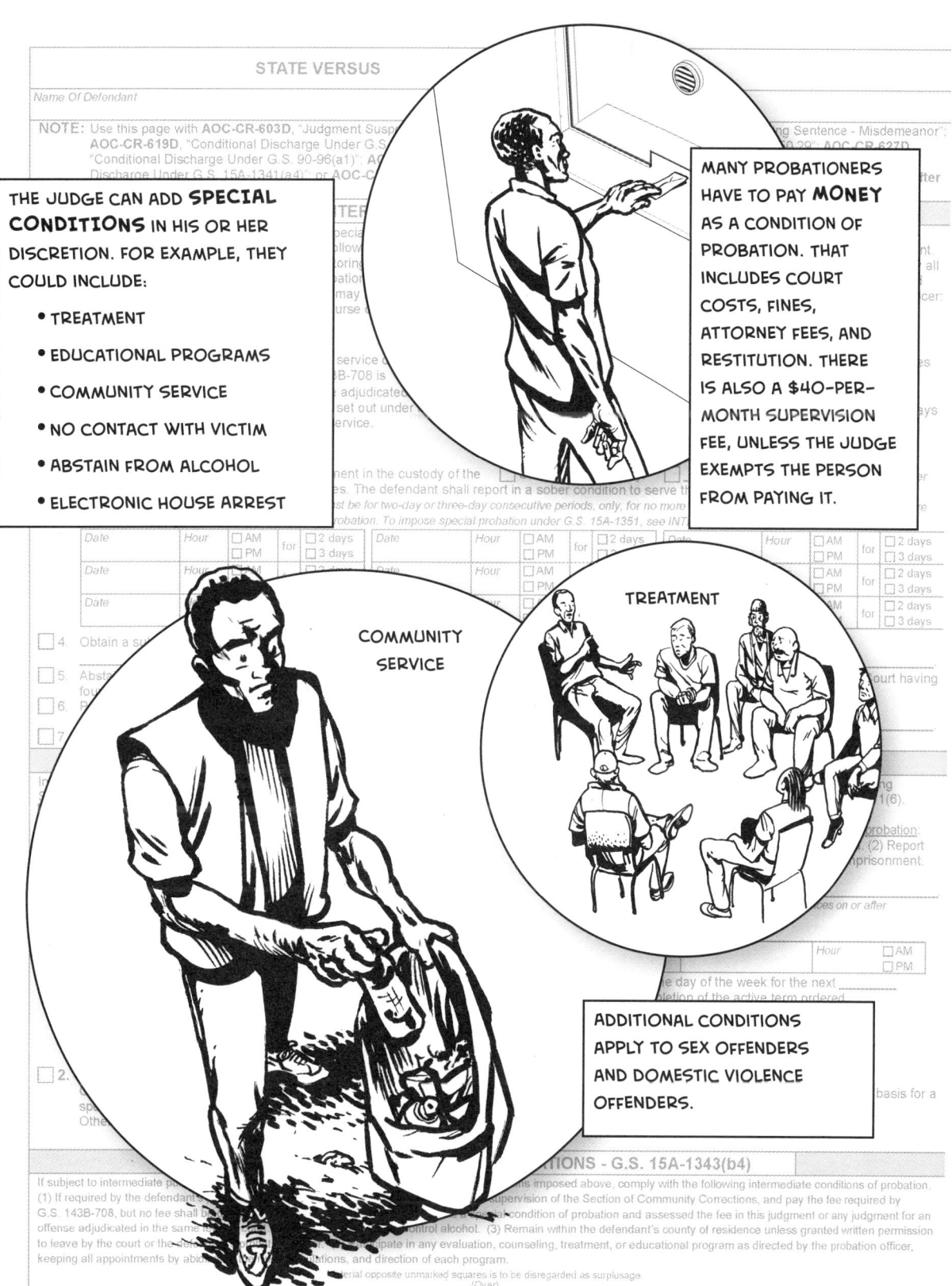

THE JUDGE CAN ADD **SPECIAL CONDITIONS** IN HIS OR HER DISCRETION. FOR EXAMPLE, THEY COULD INCLUDE:

- TREATMENT
- EDUCATIONAL PROGRAMS
- COMMUNITY SERVICE
- NO CONTACT WITH VICTIM
- ABSTAIN FROM ALCOHOL
- ELECTRONIC HOUSE ARREST

MANY PROBATIONERS HAVE TO PAY **MONEY** AS A CONDITION OF PROBATION. THAT INCLUDES COURT COSTS, FINES, ATTORNEY FEES, AND RESTITUTION. THERE IS ALSO A $40-PER-MONTH SUPERVISION FEE, UNLESS THE JUDGE EXEMPTS THE PERSON FROM PAYING IT.

COMMUNITY SERVICE

TREATMENT

ADDITIONAL CONDITIONS APPLY TO SEX OFFENDERS AND DOMESTIC VIOLENCE OFFENDERS.

SUBSTANCE ABUSE TREATMENT

SOME PROBATIONERS ARE ORDERED TO COMPLETE SUBSTANCE ABUSE TREATMENT. THAT WILL OFTEN BEGIN WITH A VISIT TO TASC (TREATMENT ACCOUNTABLILITY FOR SAFER COMMUNITIES), WHICH CONDUCTS ASSESSMENTS AND MAKES REFERRALS TO TREATMENT PROVIDERS ACROSS THE STATE.

PROBATIONERS WITH SERIOUS SUBSTANCE ABUSE ISSUES MIGHT BE ORDERED TO ATTEND AND COMPLETE ONE OF THE STATE'S TWO 90-DAY RESIDENTIAL CHEMICAL DEPENDENCY PROGRAMS: DART CHERRY FOR MEN AND THE BLACK MOUNTAIN SUBSTANCE ABUSE TREATMENT CENTER FOR WOMEN. THOSE 90-DAY PROGRAMS ARE AVAILABLE AT NO CHARGE TO PROBATIONERS WHOSE TASC ASSESSMENT INDICATES A NEED FOR RESIDENTIAL TREATMENT.

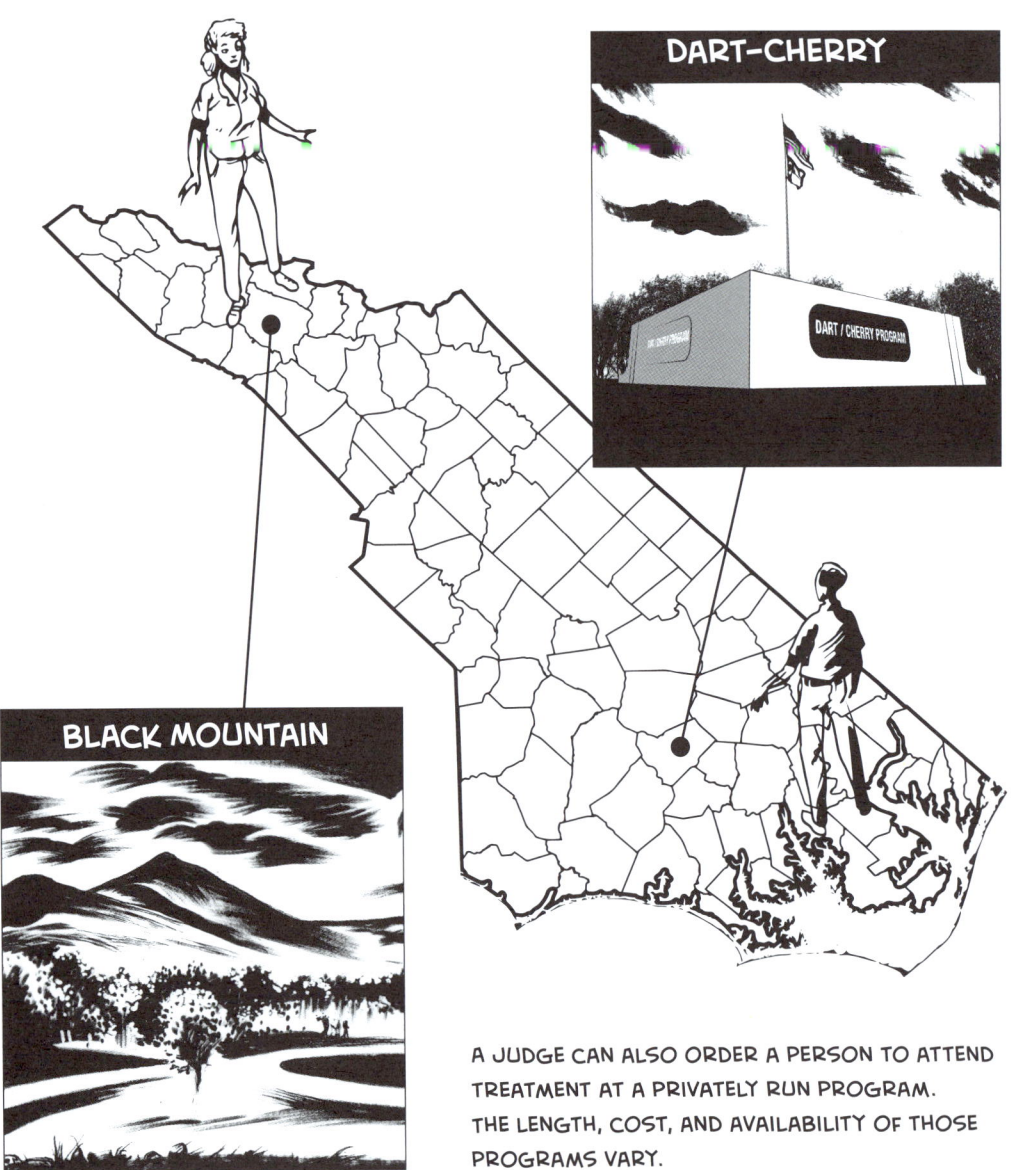

DART-CHERRY

DART / CHERRY PROGRAM

BLACK MOUNTAIN

A JUDGE CAN ALSO ORDER A PERSON TO ATTEND TREATMENT AT A PRIVATELY RUN PROGRAM. THE LENGTH, COST, AND AVAILABILITY OF THOSE PROGRAMS VARY.

NONCOMPLIANCE

OF COURSE, NOT EVERY PROBATIONER COMPLETES SUPERVISION PERFECTLY. SOME PROBATIONERS COMMIT **SERIOUS VIOLATIONS,** LIKE COMMITTING A NEW CRIME OR ABSCONDING. SOME COMMIT **TECHNICAL VIOLATIONS,** LIKE FAILING TO PAY COSTS OR FINES, TESTING POSITIVE FOR DRUGS, OR MISSING MEETINGS WITH THEIR PROBATION OFFICER.

IF THE PROBATION OFFICER THINKS THAT A PROBATIONER HAS VIOLATED A CONDITION OF SUPERVISION, THERE ARE MANY WAYS THE OFFICER CAN RESPOND.

FIRST, THE OFFICER MIGHT USE WHAT IS KNOWN AS **DELEGATED AUTHORITY,** A LAW THAT ALLOWS THE OFFICER TO IMPOSE CERTAIN ADDITIONAL CONDITIONS WITHOUT A COURT ORDER. THOSE CONDITIONS INCLUDE THINGS LIKE COMMUNITY SERVICE, TREATMENT, OR AN ELECTRONICALLY-MONITORED CURFEW. IN CASES INVOLVING "HIGH RISK" PROBATIONERS, THE OFFICER CAN ADD CERTAIN CONDITIONS EVEN WITHOUT AN ALLEGATION OF VIOLATION.

DELEGATED AUTHORITY CAN ALSO INCLUDE A 2- OR 3-DAY PERIOD OF CONFINEMENT IN THE JAIL KNOWN AS A "QUICK DIP," BUT ONLY IF THE PROBATIONER WAIVES THE RIGHT TO A HEARING ON THE VIOLATION.

VIOLATION REPORT

ALTERNATIVELY, THE PROBATION OFFICER CAN FILE A **VIOLATION REPORT** WITH THE COURT TO BRING THE VIOLATION IN FRONT OF A JUDGE. DEPENDING ON THE NATURE OF THE VIOLATION, THE OFFICER CAN EITHER CITE THE PROBATIONER TO COURT FOR A HEARING OR ARREST THE PROBATIONER. IF THE PERSON IS ARRESTED, HE OR SHE IS TAKEN BEFORE A MAGISTRATE OR OTHER JUDICIAL OFFICIAL TO DETERMINE CONDITIONS OF RELEASE (LIKE A BAIL BOND, FOR EXAMPLE). IF THE PROBATIONER IS UNABLE TO SATISFY THE CONDITIONS OF RELEASE, HE OR SHE WILL BE HELD IN THE JAIL PENDING A VIOLATION HEARING.

PROBATIONERS ARE ENTITLED TO A **PRELIMINARY HEARING** ON THE ALLEGED VIOLATION WITHIN SEVEN WORKING DAYS OF THEIR ARREST, WHERE A JUDGE WILL DETERMINE WHETHER THERE IS PROBABLE CAUSE THAT A VIOLATION OCCURRED.

PROBATION VIOLATION HEARING

IF THE PROBATIONER DOES NOT ADMIT TO THE ALLEGED
VIOLATIONS, THERE WILL BE A PROBATION VIOLATION
HEARING. A PROBATION VIOLATION HEARING IS NOT A TRIAL.
IT IS MUCH LESS FORMAL. THE PROBATIONER IS ENTITLED TO
A LAWYER IF HE OR SHE IS INDIGENT, BUT THERE IS NO JURY,
AND THE RULES OF EVIDENCE DO NOT APPLY. BASED ON EVIDENCE
PRESENTED BY THE PROSECUTOR AND THE PROBATION OFFICER,
THE JUDGE DECIDES WHETHER THE DEFENDANT VIOLATED HIS OR HER
PROBATION.

IF THE JUDGE FINDS THAT NO VIOLATION OCCURRED, THEN THE
VIOLATION WILL BE DISMISSED AND THE DEFENDANT WILL CONTINUE ON
PROBATION.

CONTINUATION

EVEN IF THERE HAS BEEN A VIOLATION, THE JUDGE CAN ALLOW THE PERSON TO CONTINUE ON PROBATION WITHOUT MAKING ANY CHANGES TO THE CONDITIONS OF SUPERVISION. THE JUDGE IS NEVER REQUIRED TO RESPOND IN ANY PARTICULAR WAY.

TERMINATION

A JUDGE CAN TERMINATE A PERSON'S PROBATION AT ANY TIME. TERMINATION MEANS THE PROBATION IS OVER AND THE PERSON NO LONGER FACES ANY CRIMINAL PUNISHMENT IN THE CASE. SOMETIMES THE JUDGE WILL SAY THAT PROBATION IS TERMINATED "UNSUCCESSFULLY" OR "UNSATISFACTORILY," BUT THOSE TERMS DON'T HAVE ANY DEFINED LEGAL MEANING, AND THE PROBATION IS STILL ENDED.

MODIFICATION

A JUDGE CAN MODIFY PROBATION TO ADD NEW CONDITIONS OR REMOVE OR CHANGE EXISTING CONDITIONS. THE JUDGE CAN ALSO MODIFY PROBATION BY TRANSFERRING A SUPERVISED PROBATIONER TO UNSUPERVISED PROBATION.

EXTENSION

A JUDGE CAN EXTEND A PERSON'S PROBATION TO AS LONG AS 5 YEARS (OR AS LONG AS 2 YEARS IN DEFERRED PROSECUTION OR CONDITIONAL DISCHARGE CASES). NORTH CAROLINA LAW ALSO ALLOWS FOR A SPECIAL TYPE OF EXTENSION OF UP TO 3 YEARS BEYOND THE ORIGINAL PERIOD OF PROBATION, BUT ONLY IF (1) THE DEFENDANT CONSENTS, (2) THE EXTENSION IS ORDERED IN THE LAST 6 MONTHS OF THE ORIGINAL PERIOD OF PROBATION, AND (3) THE EXTENSION IS TO ALLOW TIME TO PAY RESTITUTION OR COMPLETE MEDICAL OR PSYCHIATRIC TREATMENT.

VIOLATION HAS OCCURRED,
ARE POSSIBLE.

CONTEMPT

WITH PROPER NOTICE AND PROOF OF A VIOLATION BEYOND A REASONABLE DOUBT, A PROBATIONER CAN BE HELD IN CONTEMPT AND JAILED FOR UP TO 30 DAYS.

QUICK DIP

THE JUDGE CAN ORDER A PERIOD OF 2 OR 3 DAYS IN THE LOCAL JAIL, SOMETIMES REFERRED TO AS A "QUICK DIP." A QUICK DIP IMPOSED BY A JUDGE IS SIMILAR TO A QUICK DIP IMPOSED BY A PROBATION OFFICER THROUGH DELEGATED AUTHORITY. QUICK DIPS ARE NOT ALLOWED IN DWI CASES.

SPLIT SENTENCE

SIMILAR TO A SPLIT SENTENCE ORDERED AT SENTENCING, A JUDGE CAN MODIFY PROBATION TO ORDER CONFINEMENT FOR UP TO ONE-FOURTH OF THE DEFENDANT'S MAXIMUM SENTENCE.

CRV

IN FELONY AND DWI CASES, THE JUDGE CAN ORDER CONFINEMENT IN RESPONSE TO VIOLATION (CRV) FOR TECHNICAL VIOLATIONS (VIOLATIONS OTHER THAN A NEW CRIME OR ABSCONDING). THE DETAILS OF CRV ARE COVERED ON THE NEXT PAGE.

CONFINEMENT IN RESPONSE TO VIOLATION (CRV)

CRV IS A PERIOD OF IMPRISONMENT IMPOSED IN RESPONSE TO A TECHNICAL VIOLATION (THE JUDGE CANNOT ORDER CRV FOR NEW CRIMES OR ABSCONDING).

FOR FELONY PROBATIONERS A CRV PERIOD IS 90 DAYS. FELONY CRV IS GENERALLY SERVED IN ONE OF THE STATE'S CRV CENTERS. THERE ARE TWO CRV CENTERS FOR MEN—ONE IN ROBESON COUNTY AND ONE IN BURKE COUNTY. THE LONE CRV CENTER FOR WOMEN IS IN DAVIDSON COUNTY AT NORTH PIEDMONT CORRECTIONAL INSTITUTION. AT A CRV CENTER, A PROBATIONER CAN EXPECT TO DO THINGS LIKE DRUG EDUCATION AND LIFE-SKILLS TRAINING.

FOR DWI PROBATIONERS, A CRV PERIOD IS "UP TO" 90 DAYS. CRV FOR A DWI IS SERVED IN A COUNTY JAIL THROUGH A PROGRAM CALLED THE STATEWIDE MISDEMEANANT CONFINEMENT PROGRAM—USUALLY THE JAIL IN THE COUNTY OF SUPERVISION, BUT SOMETIMES IN A NEARBY COUNTY.

CRV IS NOT ALLOWED FOR MISDEMEANOR PROBATIONERS, UNLESS IT IS AN OLDER CASE WHERE THE PERSON WAS PLACED ON PROBATION BEFORE DECEMBER 1, 2015. IN THOSE CASES, CRV CAN BE UP TO 90 DAYS OR THE LENGTH OF THE SUSPENDED SENTENCE, WHICHEVER IS LESS.

UPON COMPLETION OF A CRV, A PROBATIONER IS GENERALLY RELEASED BACK TO THE COUNTY OF SUPERVISION TO CONTINUE ON PROBATION. HOWEVER, YOU MIGHT ALSO HEAR THE PHRASE "**TERMINAL CRV.**" THAT IS A SITUATION WHERE THE CRV IS THE LAST THING THAT HAPPENS IN THE PROBATION CASE, EITHER BECAUSE (1) THE CRV USES UP ALL OF THE TIME REMAINING ON THE PROBATIONER'S SUSPENDED TERM OF IMPRISONMENT, (2) THE PERIOD OF PROBATION EXPIRES BEFORE THE CRV ENDS, OR (3) THE JUDGE ORDERS THAT THE CASE IS TERMINATED AFTER THE PERSON COMPLETES THE CRV.

A PROBATIONER CAN NEVER RECEIVE MORE THAN TWO CRVS IN A PARTICULAR CASE. AFTER TWO CRVS, THE PERSON CAN BE REVOKED FOR ANY LATER VIOLATION.

REVOCATION

REVOCATION MEANS A PROBATIONER'S SUSPENDED TERM OF IMPRISONMENT IS ACTIVATED AND HE OR SHE IS SENT TO PRISON OR JAIL.

SERIOUS VIOLATIONS

TWO PROBATION CONDITIONS ARE ELIGIBLE FOR REVOCATION UPON FIRST VIOLATION:

- COMMITTING A **NEW CRIMINAL OFFENSE** WHILE ON PROBATION

- **ABSCONDING** (AVOIDING SUPERVISION OR MAKING YOUR WHEREABOUTS UNKNOWN)

THE JUDGE IS NOT **REQUIRED** TO REVOKE PROBATION FOR THOSE VIOLATIONS, BUT HE OR SHE COULD.

TECHNICAL VIOLATIONS

FOR VIOLATIONS OF ALL OTHER CONDITIONS, A PERSON CANNOT BE REVOKED ON HIS OR HER FIRST VIOLATION. INSTEAD, NORTH CAROLINA LAW TAKES A **THREE STRIKES** APPROACH.

- **FELONY AND DWI** PROBATIONERS CANNOT BE REVOKED FOR A TECHNICAL VIOLATION UNLESS THEY HAVE SERVED **TWO CRVS** IMPOSED FOR PRIOR TECHNICAL VIOLATIONS.

- **MISDEMEANOR** PROBATIONERS CANNOT BE REVOKED FOR A TECHNICAL VIOLATION UNLESS THEY HAVE SERVED **TWO QUICK DIPS** IMPOSED IN RESPONSE TO PRIOR TECHNICAL VIOLATIONS, EITHER BY A JUDGE OR BY A PROBATION OFFICER THROUGH DELEGATED AUTHORITY.

IF THE JUDGE REVOKES PROBATION, AN ACTIVATED FELONY SENTENCE IS SERVED AS DESCRIBED IN ISSUE NO. 1 OF THIS SERIES, "IN PRISON: SERVING A FELONY SENTENCE IN NORTH CAROLINA." ONCE THE TERM OF IMPRISONMENT IS SERVED AS DESCRIBED IN THAT BOOK, THE INMATE WILL BE RELEASED TO POST-RELEASE SUPERVISION FOR 9 MONTHS (FOR CLASS F–I FELONIES), 12 MONTHS (FOR CLASS B1–E FELONIES), OR 60 MONTHS (FOR ANY CRIME REQUIRING SEX OFFENDER REGISTRATION).

REVOKED MISDEMEANOR AND DWI SENTENCES ARE GENERALLY SERVED IN A COUNTY JAIL.

ABOUT 20 PERCENT OF ALL PROBATION CASES END WITH REVOCATION.

EXPIRATION

IF A PROBATIONER MAKES IT TO THE END OF THE PROBATION
PERIOD WITHOUT GETTING REVOKED, PROBATION **EXPIRES**
AND THE CASE ENDS. ONCE THE CASE EXPIRES OR IS TERMINATED,
NO FURTHER VIOLATIONS CAN BE ALLEGED AND THERE IS NO
POSSIBILITY OF THE SUSPENDED TERM OF IMPRISONMENT BEING
ACTIVATED. FELONY PROBATIONERS WILL HAVE THEIR CITIZENSHIP
RIGHTS RESTORED, INCLUDING THE RIGHT TO VOTE.

THE SENTENCE IS COMPLETE.